GRYFFINDOR

SLYTHERIN

RAVENCLAW

HUFFLEPUFF

Producer's Note

"Hello, I'm David Heyman, the producer on all the Harry Potter™ films. Now that you have visited *Harry Potter: The Exhibition*, I hope you'll take a moment to enjoy the artefacts and accompanying content featured in this companion book. Inside the following pages, you'll see a one-of-a-kind collection of props, costumes, and other artefacts that have been created by a collection of artists and craftspeople. On behalf of all the people who have worked on the *Harry Potter* films, we hope you'll enjoy this book."

Harry Potter in the Movies

Hogwarts™ Arrival

Each year, dozens of witches and wizards travel from London to *Hogwarts* via the Hogwarts Express. The train stops at Hogsmeade™ Station, where Rubeus Hagrid™, Keeper of Keys and Grounds at *Hogwarts*, escorts the first-years to the castle via a fleet of small boats, and returning students climb into carriages that will take them to the castle.

FLYING FORD ANGLIA
Left and below: The Flying Ford Anglia transported Harry and Ron to *Hogwarts* just before their second year after they missed the Hogwarts Express.

7990 TD

"(We had) sixteen cars. They came in all sorts of colours. But we had to... match them all up. We had wing mirrors and wheels and wheel trims... coming out of our ears."
—John Richardson, Special Effects Supervisor

Gryffindor™ Common Room

The *Gryffindor* common room can be found in one of the *Hogwarts* castle's towers. *Gryffindor* students spend much of their time in their common room when not in class. It is decorated in Gryffindor's colours of scarlet and gold.

WANDS
Below: Harry Potter's wand (top) - made of holly with a phoenix feather core from Fawkes's tail - and Hermione Granger's wand (middle). Ron Weasley's wand (bottom) was broken when he and Harry crashed the flying car into the Whomping Willow™ during *Harry Potter and the Chamber of Secrets*.

WIZARD MONEY
Above: Wizard currency, including Galleons, Sickles and Knuts.

"Harry's wand is iconic. It's what you see nearly every time you see him... (Wands) are, more than any other piece in the film, a demonstration of the owner's character."
-Pierre Bohanna, Head of Department: Modeler

QUIDDITCH™ BOARD GAME

Above: *Gryffindor* students study, relax, and play games, such as this *Quidditch* board game, in their common room.

"That was a pretty significant moment, casting Harry, Ron, and Hermione. (Those characters are) the heart of these films – more than the visual effects, more than anything, more than the fantasy. It's those kids (who) make the story feel real and relatable."

-David Heyman, Producer

HARRY POTTER'S TRUNK

Above: Harry Potter's trunk contains an assortment of chocolates spiked with love potion (given to him during his sixth year by Romilda Vane), his glasses, Marauder's Map, his *Hogwarts* acceptance letter, and a photo album with pictures of his parents.

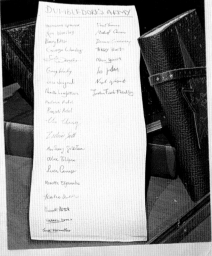

DUMBLEDORE'S ARMY™ PARCHMENT

Left: The parchment signed in the Hog's Head pub by students who enlisted as members of *Dumbledore's Army* - as seen in *Harry Potter and the Order of the Phoenix.*

HARRY POTTER'S GLASSES

Far left: Glasses worn by *Harry Potter* (Daniel Radcliffe) which were fixed more than once by *Hermione Granger* as seen in the *Harry Potter* films.

Gryffindor Boys' Dormitory

Harry shares a dormitory room with four other *Gryffindor* boys in his year. The room has five large four-poster beds with scarlet draping that is patterned with astrological signs, unicorns, and stars; bevelled-glass windows; and trunks to hold the boys' personal belongings.

GOLDEN EGG

Right: The golden egg retrieved by *Harry Potter* from the clutches of the Hungarian Horntail dragon during the first task of the Triwizard Tournament™.

GRYFFINDOR NOTICEBOARD

Above: The noticeboard, as seen in the *Gryffindor* common room in the *Harry Potter* films.

BETWEEN TAKES

Right: Daniel Radcliffe and Rupert Grint laugh between takes while filming *Harry Potter and the Half-Blood Prince*.

HARRY'S SCHOOL UNIFORM

Above: The school uniform worn by *Harry Potter* (Daniel Radcliffe) as seen in *Harry Potter and the Order of the Phoenix*. *Harry Potter* is known as "the boy who lived" after Lord Voldemort™ attempted to kill him as a baby.

MARAUDER'S MAP

Above: In his dormitory, Harry (Daniel Radcliffe) studies the Marauder's Map. Hedwig™, his owl, is perched by his side. The map was given to Harry by Fred and George Weasley during Harry's third year at *Hogwarts*.

RON AND HARRY

Below: Ron (Rupert Grint) and Harry (Daniel Radcliffe) in *Harry Potter and The Goblet of Fire*.

HARRY'S ACCEPTANCE LETTER

Above: One of many acceptance letters to *Hogwarts* School of Witchcraft and Wizardry delivered to Harry in *Harry Potter and the Philosopher's Stone*.

HERMIONE GRANGER'S CASUAL CLOTHES AND SCHOOL UNIFORM

Casual clothing worn by *Hermione Granger* (Emma Watson) when punching *Draco Malfoy* and rescuing *Buckbeak* in *Harry Potter and the Prisoner of Azkaban*, and the school uniform worn by *Hermione Granger* in *Harry Potter and the Order of the Phoenix*. Hermione is one of Harry's best friends, and despite being born of Muggle parents, she is one of the brightest witches of her age.

"The Time-Turner™ essentially... is like a piece of jewellery... I wish I had one sometimes."
-Pierre Bohanna, Head of Department: Modeller

TIME-TURNER

Above: The *Time-Turner*, which takes its user back one hour with each turn of the hourglass, was used by Hermione to take additional classes at *Hogwarts* during her third year. Below left: Harry (Daniel Radcliffe) and Hermione (Emma Watson) use the *Time-Turner* to travel back in time and save Sirius Black™ and Buckbeak™ in *Harry Potter and the Prisoner of Azkaban*.

LOVE POTION CHOCOLATES

Right: Box containing love potion-spiked chocolates from Romilda Vane intended for Harry, but eaten by Ron, in *Harry Potter and the Half-Blood Prince*.

RON WEASLEY'S SCHOOL UNIFORM

Below: The school uniform worn by *Ron Weasley* (Rupert Grint) as seen in *Harry Potter and the Order of the Phoenix*. Ron is one of Harry's best friends, and an avid wizard chess player.

RON WEASLEY'S SWEATER

Above: The monogrammed sweater worn by *Ron Weasley* (Rupert Grint) on the Hogwarts Express in *Harry Potter and the Goblet of Fire*.

RON WEASLEY'S TRUNK

Left: A collection of items from Ron Weasley's trunk - including a copy of *Seeker Weekly*; various items celebrating Ron's favourite *Quidditch* team, the Chudley Cannons; and the Howler™ sent to Ron by Mrs. Weasley in *Harry Potter and the Chamber of Secrets*, admonishing him for stealing his father's flying car.

COMMON ROOM ITEMS

Items in the common room include the dress shoes worn by Neville as he practised his dance steps for the Yule Ball in *Harry Potter and the Goblet of Fire*, as well as various items that appeared throughout the *Harry Potter* films - wizard money (Galleons, Sickles, Knuts), pumpkin juice bottles, periodicals like the Daily Prophet™ and *The Quibbler*, and assorted wands.

NEVILLE LONGBOTTOM'S BATTLE CLOTHES

Below and right: Torn and bloodied clothing worn by Neville Longbottom™ (Matthew Lewis), in the final battle scene from *Harry Potter and the Deathly Hallows – Part 2*.

NEVILLE LONGBOTTOM'S MIMBULUS MIMBLETONIA AND PRUNING KIT

Left: Neville, loyal friend to *Harry Potter* and fellow *Gryffindor*, has a passion for Herbology. Top: Next to Neville's shoes are his Mimbulus mimbletonia and related pruning kit from *Harry Potter and the Order of the Phoenix*.

LUNA LOVEGOOD'S CLOTHING

Left: Casual clothing worn by Luna Lovegood™ (Evanna Lynch), as worn for a scene on the Hogwarts Express in *Harry Potter and the Deathly Hallows – Part 1*.

LUNA LOVEGOOD'S SPECTRESPECS (AND THE QUIBBLER)

Left, above and below: Spectrespecs worn by *Luna Lovegood* in *Harry Potter and the Half-Blood Prince*. The Spectrespecs, which were given away with *The Quibbler*, enable Luna to see *Wrackspurts* and find Harry under his Invisibility Cloak after he's been cursed by *Draco Malfoy*.

Hogwarts Classes

The Potions classroom at *Hogwarts* is located in the dungeons. It is dark and colder than the rest of the castle. Each student has their own cauldron in which they learn how to brew all sorts of solutions, draughts, and elixirs. The Divination classroom is located at the top of *Hogwarts'* North Tower – and looks more like a cross between someone's attic and an old-fashioned teashop than a classroom. Divination students use tea leaves and crystal balls, among other things, in an effort to predict the future. Herbology classes take place in the greenhouses behind *Hogwarts* castle. Here, students learn all about magical plants—which become more interesting and dangerous each year of study.

PROFESSOR SPROUT'S ROBES
Robes (foreground) worn by Herbology Professor Pomona Sprout – who taught students about Mandrakes. Behind the robes are Mandrakes re-potted by the Slytherin™ and Gryffindor Herbology class in *Harry Potter and the Chamber of Secrets*.

PROFESSOR TRELAWNEY'S ROBES
Left and below: Robes worn by Divination Professor Sybill Trelawney (Emma Thompson) in *Harry Potter and the Order of the Phoenix*. Professor Trelawney is the Seer who made the prophecy about *Harry Potter* and *Lord Voldemort*.

CRYSTAL BALL
Far right: Harry (Daniel Radcliffe) and Ron (Rupert Grint) attempt to see the future in Divination class using a crystal ball.

POTIONS PROFESSORS' ROBES

Below: Robes worn by Potions professors Horace Slughorn in *Harry Potter and the Half-Blood Prince* (left) and Severus Snape™ throughout the film series (right).

POTIONS ITEMS

Above: Items from Professor Slughorn's Potions classroom, including the vial used to hold the Felix Felicis potion and the box containing bezoars, as seen in *Harry Potter and the Half-Blood Prince*.

POTIONS TEXTBOOKS

Right: Copies of *Advanced Potion-Making* and *Magical Crafts and Potions*. *Severus Snape* was the Potions master during Harry's first five years at *Hogwarts*. During Harry's sixth year, Horace Slughorn took over the post - and Harry began to excel in the subject...although his success was largely due to his copy of *Advanced Potion-Making*, previously owned by the Half-Blood Prince™.

"We painted a life-size portrait of (Gilderoy Lockhart™) painting himself, and filled the rest of the rooms with photographs of him doing impossible sporting things, quite unlike his real character."

-Stephenie McMillan, Set Decorator

Defence Against The Dark Arts

Students at *Hogwarts* learn to defend themselves against Dark Magic in the Defence Against the Dark Arts classroom – which contains a number of magical artefacts used during lessons. Rumour has it that the post of Defence Against the Dark Arts professor has been jinxed since Dumbledore™ refused to give it to Tom Riddle™ (now *Lord Voldemort*) years ago. No professor has lasted longer than a year in the position since then.

– Professor Lockhart –

DARK ARTS ITEMS
Left: A Defence Against the Dark Arts General Knowledge test with various personal questions about Professor Lockhart, and Lockhart's wand, publicity shots, and stationery set.

CORNISH PIXIES
Below: Cornish pixies were released in the Defence Against the Dark Arts classroom by Professor *Gilderoy Lockhart* in *Harry Potter and the Chamber of Secrets*. Lockhart, who taught during Harry's second year, ended his career at *Hogwarts* when he was hit with his own Memory Charm.

TRAVELS WITH TROLLS
Above: One of Gilderoy Lockhart's published works, *Travels with Trolls*, given to *Harry Potter* as a gift in Flourish and Blotts™ at the beginning of *Harry Potter and the Chamber of Secrets*.

PROFESSOR LOCKHART'S ROBES
Left, above and right: Robes worn by Professor *Gilderoy Lockhart* (Kenneth Branagh) while teaching his first Defence Against the Dark Arts class in *Harry Potter and the Chamber of Secrets*.

- Professor Lupin -

PROFESSOR LUPIN'S ROBES

Left and bottom left: Robes worn by Defence Against the Dark Arts Professor Remus Lupin (David Thewlis) in *Harry Potter and the Prisoner of Azkaban*.

PROFESSOR LUPIN'S CLASSROOM

Below left: Various items from Professor Lupin's Defence Against the Dark Arts classroom, including Lupin's wand, a book about Dark Forces, and gramophone records.

JACK-IN-THE-BOX

Top: The giant jack-in-the-box as seen in Professor Lupin's lesson on Boggarts™.

GIANT SPIDER

Above: The giant spider seen by *Ron Weasley* when confronting the *Boggart* in Defence Against the Dark Arts.

WARDROBE

The wardrobe in which the *Boggart* was kept in *Harry Potter and the Prisoner of Azkaban*. *Boggarts* take the shape of whatever a person most fears.

"Dolores Umbridge™ is all about pink... We used some mohair, we used some angora on the sweaters – anything which was contrary (to) her character. What I decided to do was to make the pink harder and harder during the film, and (finish with) an atrocious pink – a pink (that) was hard to look at. And that was my way of making her meaner and meaner."

–Jany Temime, Costume Designer

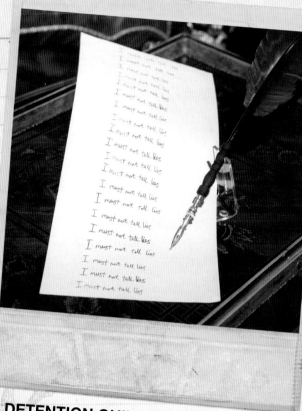

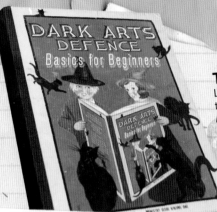

TEXTBOOK

Left: An old Dark Arts textbook, handed out by *Dolores Umbridge* in her first Defence Against the Dark Arts class.

DETENTION QUILL

Above: Paper and "special" quill given to *Harry Potter* by Professor Umbridge™ to use for his detention in *Harry Potter and the Order of the Phoenix*. The quill carved the line "I must not tell lies" into the back of Harry's hand.

PORTRAIT AND WAND

Left: A framed portrait of Minister Fudge (Robert Hardy) displayed in Umbridge's office next to her wand. The Minister for Magic sent *Dolores Umbridge* to *Hogwarts* to teach Defence Against the Dark Arts and to spy on Professor Dumbledore™.

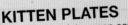

HARRY POTTER'S DECOY DETONATOR

Above: Decoy Detonator used by *Harry Potter* in *Harry Potter and the Deathly Hallows – Part 1*. The Decoy Detonator provides a distraction that enables Harry to break into Dolores Umbridge's office at the Ministry of Magic.

KITTEN PLATES

Right: Kitten plates seen covering the walls of Professor Umbridge's very pink office.

PROFESSOR UMBRIDGE'S CLOTHING

Above and opposite: Dress and jacket worn by Defence Against the Dark Arts *Professor Dolores Umbridge* (Imelda Staunton) at the start-of-term feast in *Harry Potter and the Order of the Phoenix* (pictured here with Michael Gambon as Dumbledore).

"(Umbridge) didn't really teach at all and hers was just purely textbook teaching. So the (class) room was completely empty, apart from the desks and the blackboard.... (But in) her office upstairs, the walls were painted in bright pink, all the furniture (was) pink, the curtains (were) pink, and of course the kitten plates on the walls scream(ed) at visitors."
-Stephenie McMillan, Set Decorator

Quidditch

Quidditch is the most popular sport in the wizarding world. A bit like soccer, it is played on broomsticks – in mid-air – with four different-sized balls: one Quaffle, which the Chasers try and get through one of the hoops; two Bludgers, which rocket around trying to knock players off their brooms; and one Golden Snitch™, which is bewitched to evade capture as long as possible. There are seven players on each side: three Chasers, who throw the Quaffle to each other and try and get it through one of the hoops to score a goal (worth ten points); two Beaters, who use small clubs called "Beater's Bats" to keep the Bludgers from knocking teammates (and themselves) off their brooms; one Keeper, who flies around his or her team's hoops to stop the other team from scoring; and one Seeker, who must catch the *Golden Snitch* and – hopefully – win the game.

"Internally, (brooms are) actually very complicated. They have a lot of aircraft-standard material such as titanium (and) heat-treated aluminums... so that they can be as fine and as thin as possible but also...cope with the strains of what the effects guys need to do with them."
—Pierre Bohanna, Head of Department: Modeller

NIMBUS 2000™
Above: Harry Potter's *Nimbus 2000* broomstick as seen in *Harry Potter and the Philosopher's Stone*.

QUIDDITCH EQUIPMENT AND RELATED ITEMS

Above: *Quidditch* crate containing a Quaffle, two Bludgers, a bat, and the *Golden Snitch*, as well as various items from the *Quidditch* World Cup, including scarves, programmes, binoculars, and periodicals.

THE *GOLDEN SNITCH*

Below and right: Harry Potter (Daniel Radcliffe) holds a *Golden Snitch*, as seen in *Harry Potter and the Philosopher's Stone.*

MADAM HOOCH'S ROBES

Above: Robes worn by Madam Rolanda Hooch (Zoë Wanamaker), the flying teacher, in *Harry Potter and the Philosopher's Stone.*

BROOMSTICKS

Right: Broomsticks as seen at the Quidditch World Cup campgrounds in *Harry Potter and the Goblet of Fire.*

QUIDDITCH ROBES

Above: Irish National robes (back left) and Viktor Krum's Bulgarian National robes (back right) worn in the *Quidditch* World Cup finals; robes worn by flying instructor Madam Hooch (front left); and *Gryffindor Quidditch* team robes worn by *Harry Potter* (middle) and *Ron Weasley* (front right).

"The *Slytherin* (*Quidditch*) players are in green. (In the sixth film), what we did to make them slightly more dangerous (was) to add some silver stripe(s) and some black stars... The black stars give them a little bit of a (Roman), fascistic, military look."

—Jany Temime, Costume Designer

HARRY POTTER'S *QUIDDITCH* ROBES

Right; *Quidditch* robes worn by *Harry Potter* (Daniel Radcliffe) during *Gryffindor* team tryouts in *Harry Potter and the Half-Blood Prince*.

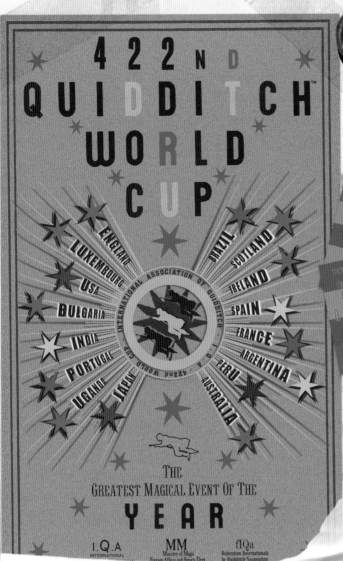

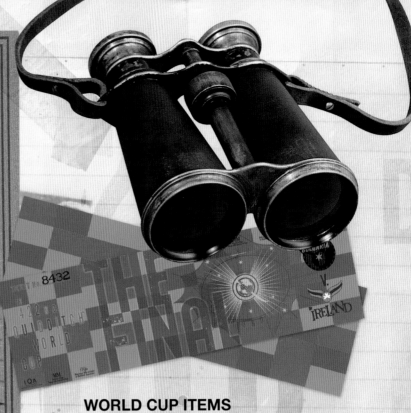

WORLD CUP ITEMS

Above and left: A *Quidditch* programme, tickets to the finals, and binoculars used at the *Quidditch* World Cup in *Harry Potter and the Goblet of Fire*.

QUIDDITCH ROBES

Below: Various *Quidditch* items, including the *Gryffindor Quidditch* robes worn by Oliver Wood (left) and *Slytherin Quidditch* robes worn by Draco Malfoy™ (right) in *Harry Potter and the Chamber of Secrets*, and the *Hufflepuff*™ *Quidditch* robes worn by Cedric Diggory (middle) in *Harry Potter and the Prisoner of Azkaban*.

Hagrid's Hut

Keeper of Keys and Grounds at *Hogwarts*, *Rubeus Hagrid* lives with his dog, Fang, in a hut on the edge of the Forbidden Forest. As *Hagrid* is half-giant, all of the furniture and many of the other items in his home are oversized.

CASUAL CLOTHING

Above and far right: The clothing worn by the executioner (far left) who came to *Hogwarts* to execute *Buckbeak* the Hippogriff, and casual clothing worn by Ron (Rupert Grint, second from left), Hermione (Emma Watson, third from left), and Harry (Daniel Radcliffe) when hiding from the executioner in the pumpkin patch just outside Hagrid's hut in *Harry Potter and the Prisoner of Azkaban*.

BUCKBEAK

Left: *Buckbeak* the Hip

HAGRID'S HUT

Inside Hagrid's hut are a massive wooden table and chairs; a stone fireplace with fireplace pokers and cooking utensils; and animal cages, baskets, and pots that hang from the walls and ceiling.

THE MONSTER BOOK OF MONSTERS

Above: A copy of *The Monster Book of Monsters*, used by members of Hagrid's Care of Magical Creatures class in *Harry Potter and the Prisoner of Azkaban*.

HAGRID'S CLOTHING

Left: *Rubeus Hagrid*, Keeper of Keys and Grounds at *Hogwarts* (Robbie Coltrane).

"For *The Monster Book of Monsters*, we had to build a book that could raise its eyes out of the cover, blink, snap its teeth, roll its tongue, and wriggle. It had to be able to squirm. Since we produced all the books for the scene with the lesson with *Hagrid*, our department had books everywhere you looked – all of them securely tied with straps, of course, because...you never know."

—Nick Dudman, Prosthetics and Make-up Effects Designer

FORBIDDEN FOREST

Left: *Harry Potter* (Daniel Radcliffe) and *Draco Malfoy* (Tom Felton) enter the Forbidden Forest with Hagrid's dog, Fang, in *Harry Potter and the Philosopher's Stone*.

LUNA AND A THESTRAL™

Above: *Luna Lovegood* (Evanna Lynch) pets a *Thestral* in *Harry Potter and the Order of the Phoenix*.

CENTAUR

Above: Centaurs, who live in the Forbidden Forest, have the legs and body of a horse and the torso, arms, and head of a man.

"The (Hungarian) Horntail Dragon is a completely (computer-generated) creature. But just because it's completely digital in its final form doesn't mean it doesn't exist at some stage as a solid object... (It's) necessary with a very big creature like (the) Horntail to (increase) the scale because you're going to scan (the) model into the computer. And you want the maximum amount of detail. So we went for the scale of the actual creature."

-Nick Dudman, Prosthetics and Make-up Effects Designer

The Forbidden Forest

The Forbidden Forest is a dark forest on the *Hogwarts* grounds. It is strictly forbidden to all pupils. Home to all types of magical creatures including unicorns, Acromantula (giant spiders), centaurs, and *Thestrals*, the Forest is well-known to *Hagrid* – who lives at its edge and teaches his Care of Magical Creatures class there.

THESTRAL
Above: A baby *Thestral*, as seen with *Luna Lovegood* in *Harry Potter and the Order of the Phoenix. Thestrals* are winged, skeletal horses that can be seen only by those who have witnessed death.

HUNGARIAN HORNTAIL DRAGON
Above: A life-sized model of the head of the Hungarian Horntail dragon. The dragon was kept in the Forbidden Forest before Harry faced it in the first task of the *Triwizard Tournament* in *Harry Potter and the Goblet of Fire.*

ACROMANTULA
Right: An Acromantula (a member of Aragog's family) encountered by Ron and Harry in the Forbidden Forest in *Harry Potter and the Chamber of Secrets.*

Dark Forces

Lord Voldemort and his followers, the Death Eaters, use Dark Magic - like the Unforgivable Curses - to gain power in the wizarding world. They have been known to use other creatures, such as Dementors™, a Basilisk, and even humans, in an attempt to secure power. Voldemort's sign - the Dark Mark- is branded onto the left arm of every Death Eater. It is also the symbol cast into the sky whenever Death Eaters have killed in Voldemort's name. Ever since Voldemort's powers were destroyed when he attempted to murder *Harry Potter* as a baby, the Dark Lord and his allies have tried to capture and kill Harry to fulfil a prophecy that would allow *Voldemort* to survive - in turn allowing him to regain his power.

DEATH EATER COSTUMES
Right: Death Eater robes and masks as seen in *Harry Potter and the Goblet of Fire*.

DEMENTOR
Below: *Dementor* on the Hogwarts Express as seen in *Harry Potter and Prisoner of Azkaban*.
Below Right: A *Dementor* attacks Harry in *Harry Potter and the Order of the Phoenix*.

"(In *Harry Potter and the Goblet of Fire*), we had silhouette(s) of (Death Eaters) appearing outside... That's why I (gave) them those black leather pointed hats, because I just wanted to have shapes, very graphic shapes, against grey sky."
- Jany Temime, Costume Designer

The Angel of Death statue used by
Wormtail™ to restrain *Harry Potter*
(Daniel Radcliffe) in the graveyard
at Little Hangleton in *Harry Potter
and the Goblet of Fire.*

DARK FORCES

Dark Forces display pieces including (from left to right) clothing worn by Draco and Lucius Malfoy; a *Dementor*; an Azkaban prison uniform; and Bellatrix Lestrange's prison uniform.

LORD VOLDEMORT'S ROBES

Right and far right: Robes worn by *Lord Voldemort* (Ralph Fiennes) during his confrontation with Harry in the graveyard in *Harry Potter and the Goblet of Fire.*

"When we did the first test on Ralph (Fiennes), he looked great (as *Lord Voldemort*). But then David Heyman.... said, 'I'd love to see him with his nose reduced.' And the minute (we did that), it stripped him of the humanity. So he's actually a perfect combination - real actor, real makeup, (and) digital manipulation."

-Nick Dudman, Prosthetics and Make-up Effects Designer

DARK FORCES

Items from *Harry Potter and the Philosopher's Stone*, including casual clothing worn by *Harry Potter*; and the robes and turban worn by Defence Against the Dark Arts Professor Quirrell as he searched for the Philosopher's Stone™ within the Mirror of Erised™.

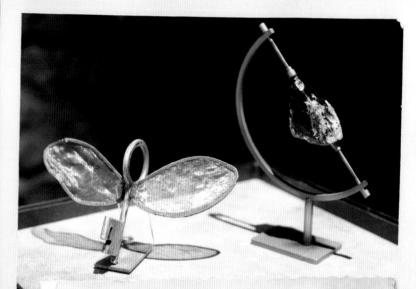

PETRIFIED COLIN CREEVEY

Above: First-year student Colin Creevey (Hugh Mitchell). Since Colin saw the Basilisk through the lens of his camera, he was merely Petrified rather than killed.
Left: Colin Creevey when he was Petrified by the Basilisk in *Harry Potter and the Chamber of Secrets*.

LORD VOLDEMORT'S WAND

Above: Lord Voldemort's wand - made of yew with a phoenix tail feather core. It is linked to Harry's wand by virtue of the fact that the same phoenix (Fawkes™) provided the feather for the core of both wands.

"We did a lot of design work on what that meant (to be Petrified) visually, and decided the best approach was to produce silicone dummies of the various people who were Petrified. And we (could) make that look like real flesh in close-up, right down to the pores in the skin and each individual hair punched in. The whole process probably (took) about two and a half months."

-Nick Dudman, Prosthetics and Make-up Effects Designer

BELLATRIX LESTRANGE'S WAND
Left: Bellatrix Lestrange's wand as seen throughout the *Harry Potter* films.

BELLATRIX LESTRANGE'S CLOTHING
Below: Clothing worn by *Bellatrix Lestrange* (Helena Bonham Carter) in *Harry Potter and the Half-Blood Prince*.

BELLATRIX LESTRANGE'S DAGGER
Above: Dagger used by *Bellatrix Lestrange* (Helena Bonham Carter) in Malfoy Manor as seen in *Harry Potter and the Deathly Hallows – Part 1*.

"The first costume (for) Bellatrix was designed (for) when... she'd just got out of Azkaban. So I thought that she had that old dress, which was ten years ago because she spent even more than ten years in Azkaban, so it had to be very damaged. And Bellatrix was a very violent person... it's a woman who really wants the destruction of Harry... she is determined, she's sexy, so I wanted her in a sort of old chic rag."

—Jany Temmie, Costume Designer

THREE OF VOLDEMORT'S HORCRUXES

Above: (Clockwise from top left) Helga Hufflepuff's cup, Rowena Ravenclaw's diadem and Salazar Slytherin's locket, as seen in the *Harry Potter* films.

RESURRECTION STONE

Top right: Harry uses the Resurrection Stone to summon *Sirius Black*, *Remus Lupin*, and his parents before facing *Voldemort* in the Forbidden Forest in *Harry Potter and the Deathly Hallows – Part 2*.

TOM RIDDLE'S DIARY AND THE BASILISK FANG

Bottom right: Tom Riddle's diary, pierced by Harry with a Basilisk fang in *Harry Potter and the Chamber of Secrets*.

The Wedding

When Bill Weasley and Fleur Delacour's wedding reception is cut short by news that Voldemort has seized control of the Ministry of Magic, Harry, Ron and Hermione Disapparate to London and begin their search for the remaining Horcruxes.

HERMIONE GRANGER'S DRESS

Above and Right: The dress worn by *Hermione Granger* (Emma Watson) at the wedding of Bill Weasley and Fleur Delacour in *Harry Potter and the Deathly Hallows - Part 1.*

HERMIONE GRANGER'S BEADED BAG

Above: The beaded bag Hermione enchants with an Undetectable Extension Charm in order to carry the trio's essentials throughout the *Harry Potter and the Deathly Hallows* films.

RON WEASLEY'S SUIT

Above: The suit worn by *Ron Weasley* (Rupert Grint) at the wedding of Bill Weasley and Fleur Delacour in *Harry Potter and the Deathly Hallows - Part 1*.

XENOPHILIUS LOVEGOOD'S CLOTHING AND DEATHLY HALLOWS NECKLACE

Above: Clothing and Deathly Hallows necklace worn by Xenophilius Lovegood (Rhys Ifans) at the wedding of Bill Weasley and Fleur Delacour in *Harry Potter and the Deathly Hallows - Part 1*.

LUNA LOVEGOOD'S DRESS

Above: The dress worn by *Luna Lovegood* (Evanna Lynch) at the wedding of Bill Weasley and Fleur Delacour in *Harry Potter and the Deathly Hallows - Part 1*.

EDUCATIONAL DECREES

Various Educational Decrees handed down by *Professor Umbridge* and posted on the walls of *Hogwarts* by Argus Filch in *Harry Potter and the Order of the Phoenix.*

Great Hall

Lit by thousands of candles that float above the room, and with a ceiling bewitched to look like the sky outside, the Great Hall at *Hogwarts* serves as the main meeting area for students – and is where students share meals and receive owl post. The start-of-term feast, Sorting Ceremony, and the end-of-term feast are held here, as are special events like the Yule Ball.

GREAT HALL
Above: *Dumbledore* greets students during the start-of-term feast in the Great Hall.

CUP AND QUILLS

The Triwizard Cup™, and the Quick-Quotes Quill and notebooks used by *Daily Prophet* reporter Rita Skeeter in *Harry Potter and the Goblet of Fire*.

DEATHLY HALLOWS™

Above (Clockwise from top): The Elder Wand is believed to be the most powerful wand in existence. In *Harry Potter and the Deathly Hallows - Part 1*, Lord Voldemort breaks into Dumbledore's tomb and steals the Elder Wand. Harry uses the Resurrection Stone to summon *Sirius Black*, *Remus Lupin*, and his parents before facing Voldemort in the Forbidden Forest in *Harry Potter and the Deathly Hallows – Part 2*. The Invisibility Cloak enables its wearer to become invisible and can be seen throughout the *Harry Potter* films. In *Harry Potter and the Deathly Hallows - Part 2*, Harry Potter and *Griphook* use the Invisibility Cloak to aid them in breaking into Gringotts.

SWEETS

Right; Sweets include Chocolate Frogs™, Exploding Bonbons, and Bertie Bott's Every-Flavour Beans™. In the films, students purchase these on the Hogwarts Express and at Honeydukes in *Hogsmeade*.

"The *Triwizard Cup*... was a really difficult piece to make, because it obviously has the metal elements but also a lot of clear quartz effect... Once we finished the first piece, we then had to go back again and replicate (it) exactly as a rubberized piece – which was difficult because clear rubber is not something you find on the shelves."
—Pierre Bohanna, Head of Department: Modeler

THE LIFE AND LIES OF ALBUS DUMBLEDORE BOOK

Left: Copy of *The Life and Lies of Albus Dumbledore* book found by *Hermione Granger* in Bathilda Bagshot's home in *Harry Potter and the Deathly Hallows – Part 1*.

DUMBLEDORE'S ROBES
Robes worn by *Hogwarts* Headmaster
Albus Dumbledore™ (Richard Harris,
seen far left) at the end-of-year feast in
Harry Potter and the Chamber of Secrets.

GREAT HALL DOORS
Above: A panel from one of the doors leading into the Great Hall; the doors are intricately carved and made of heavy wood.

SCHOOL UNIFORMS AND *GOBLET OF FIRE* CASKET
Right: Items seen in *Harry Potter and the Goblet of Fire*, including the casket used to carry the *Goblet of Fire* and school uniforms worn by the Triwizard champions.

"Because I'm French myself, I think the worst thing (that) can happen to a French girl is to be (in) the rain in Scotland... The (Beauxbatons girls) look so soft and completely (not) adapted to the climate. And that's what I wanted to show."

— Jany Temime, Costume Designer

VIKTOR KRUM'S SCHOOL UNIFORM
Above left: Durmstrang school uniform worn by Triwizard champion Viktor Krum (Stanislav Ianevski).

FLEUR DELACOUR'S SCHOOL UNIFORM
Above: Beauxbatons school uniform worn by Triwizard champion Fleur Delacour (Clémence Poésy).

EXAMS AND REPORTS
Bottom: Ordinary Wizarding Levels (O.W.L.) test papers and study guides as seen in *Harry Potter and the Order of the Phoenix*, and general progress reports. The subject-specific O.W.L. examinations are taken at the end of a student's fifth year at *Hogwarts*.

SIRIUS BLACK'S CLOTHING

Left and below: Clothing worn by *Sirius Black* (Gary Oldman), Harry Potter's godfather and a member of the Order of the Phoenix™, at the Order's Grimmauld Place headquarters.

HAVE YOU SEEN THIS WIZARD?

AZKABAN PRISON

APPROACH WITH EXTREME CAUTION!
DO NOT ATTEMPT TO USE
MAGIC AGAINST THIS MAN!

Any information leading to the arrest of this
man shall be duly rewarded

Notify immediately by owl the Ministry of Magic

SIRIUS BLACK'S WAND

Above: Sirius Black's wand, as seen throughout the *Harry Potter* films.

SIRIUS BLACK 'WANTED POSTER'

Above: In *Harry Potter and the Prisoner of Azkaban*, *Sirius Black* 'Wanted' posters were displayed in Hogsmeade following his escape from Azkaban. Sirius was a member of the Order of the Phoenix, and Harry Potter's godfather.

FAWKES

Above: Dumbledore's phoenix, *Fawkes*, as seen throughout the *Harry Potter* films.

GREAT HALL

Right: Filius Flitwick (Warwick Davis), the Charms professor and Head of Ravenclaw™ house, conducts the *Hogwarts* school choir during the Yule Ball in the Great Hall.

YULE BALL ITEMS

Left: Various items from the Yule Ball as seen in *Harry Potter and the Goblet of Fire*, including an ice-sculpture-centrepiece, Christmas crackers, place settings, platters, a table cloth, and Yule Ball programmes, and invitations.

YULE BALL ROBES

Right: Dress robes worn by *Ron Weasley* (Rupert Grint) to the Yule Ball in *Harry Potter and the Goblet of Fire*.

YULE BALL ATTIRE

Top and top left: Gown worn by *Hermione Granger* (Emma Watson) and dress robes worn by Viktor Krum (Stanislav Ianevski) of Durmstrang, one of the four Triwizard champions, to the Yule Ball. Above, left and centre: Dress worn by Cho Chang (Katie Leung) and dress robes worn by Hogwarts champion Cedric Diggory (Robert Pattinson) to the Yule Ball.

HERMIONE'S EARRINGS

Left: Hermione's earrings, worn to the Yule Ball, as seen in *Harry Potter and the Goblet of Fire*.

"One of the most exciting sets of all the films was the transformation of the Great Hall for the Yule Ball in the *Goblet of Fire*. We covered all the walls with silver fabric and hung matching silver curtains (on) all the windows, (using) literally thousands of meters of fabric. The stone gargoyles and lamps were turned to silver... Best of all were the magical ice sculptures on the food and drinks tables. The whole operation took several weeks and had to be organised like a military manoeuvre."
-Stephenie McMillan, Set Decorator

YULE BALL ATTIRE

Above: Dress robes worn by *Albus Dumbledore* (above left) and Professor *Minerva McGonagall*™ (above right) at the Yule Ball in *Harry Potter and the Goblet of Fire*. In the centre are Dumbledore's other dress robes, worn to various events in the Great Hall.

YULE BALL

Right: Professors *Snape*™ (Alan Rickman), *McGonagall* (Maggie Smith), and *Dumbledore* (Michael Gambon) enjoy the festivities of the Yule Ball.

GODRIC GRYFFINDOR'S SWORD

Right: Once owned by Hogwarts founder *Godric Gryffindor*, the sword of Gryffindor is said to present itself to any worthy Gryffindor. The sword is first seen in *Harry Potter and the Chamber of Secrets* when Harry uses it to slay the Basilisk. The sword becomes invaluable to Harry and his friends for the destruction of Horcruxes in the *Harry Potter and the Deathly Hallows* films.

"(For Professor McGonagall's Yule Ball robes), I found that great fabric that had a... zigzag design. And when (it) pleated, (it) pleated like a shell. And that (made) it very snakelike. So it was really witchy."
– Jany Temime, Costume Designer

DUMBLEDORE'S WAND

Above: Headmaster Dumbledore's wand, as seen throughout the *Harry Potter* films.

Artefacts & Artisans

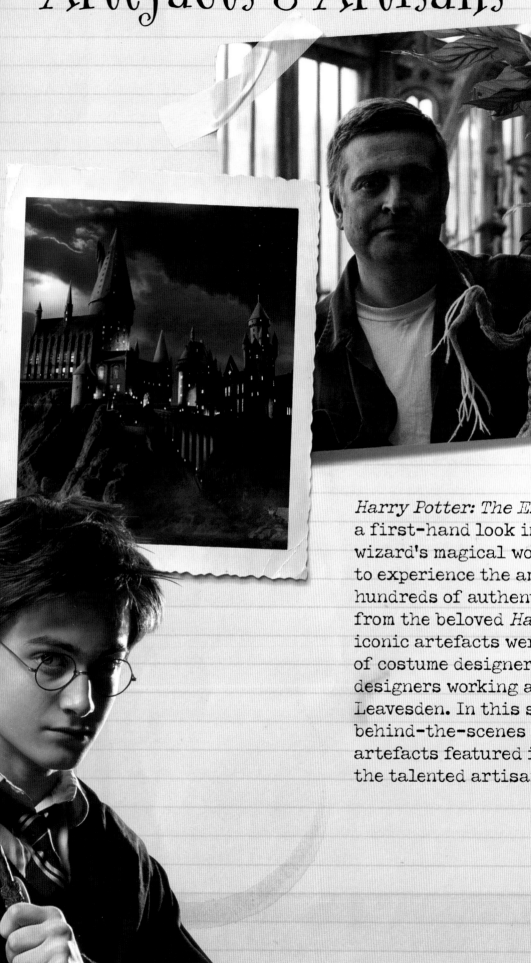

Harry Potter: The Exhibition offers guests a first-hand look inside the famous wizard's magical world and the opportunity to experience the amazing craftsmanship of hundreds of authentic costumes and props from the beloved *Harry Potter* films. These iconic artefacts were created by a team of costume designers, prop masters and set designers working at Warner Bros. Studios, Leavesden. In this section, you will find behind-the-scenes information about the artefacts featured in the exhibition and the talented artisans that created them.

Costumes

RON'S SWEATER
JANY TEMIME: "Everybody loves Ron because Ron is such an underdog and such a hero. He's a wonderful, wonderful character. So I created Ron's sweater for the film number three, just putting an R on top of the sweater, thinking that his mom would have knitted it for him. You know, in the beginning you always wear what Mum gives you. And then when your mum has bad taste you're really unlucky! [Laughs] That's what happened to him! Mum has really bad taste. And he still carries it. And he's still likable, whatever he wears."

HERMIONE'S YULE BALL DRESS
JANY TEMIME: "That was a very difficult dress. Hermione is suddenly seen as something other than a jeans and tee-shirt girl. She had to have the potential but not be an adult. When we did the ball dress she was really young and it is very difficult for a gorgeous girl like Hermione to have to wear a long evening dress and still look like a little girl. But it worked."

VOLDEMORT COSTUME
JANY TEMIME: "*Voldemort* had different costumes. He had costumes when he's just born, reborn. We used lots of very thin silk to give that idea of something just starting…almost like a membrane, you know? And then the second costume, we just give to the old character a little bit more presence. He is more – he is there. And he is starting [to get] his strength, by adding an extra layer of heavier silk."

Sets

HOGWARTS CASTLE
STUART CRAIG: "The inspiration behind the castle wasn't one single image that we saw…it came from a process of discovery. We said, *Hogwarts* is, what, how old? Over a thousand years old. What institutions in Europe are that kind of age? So that's where we went. And it gave us a kind of bedrock of authenticity…. we didn't want to make it whimsical. It just seemed that the magic would be more powerful if it grew out of something that was seemingly very real."

HAGRID'S HUT
STUART CRAIG: "I think the biggest challenge I had was about Hagrid's hut from an eight-year-old girl, who said, "But Hagrid's hut isn't made of stone. It's made of wood!" And of course she's right [laughs]! It is in the book. And I rather lamely said, "Yes, but we do have a wooden floor and we do have a wooden roof, so it can burn." So, that's a pretty serious challenge. The fact that we've had so few is gratifying."

Props

HARRY'S GLASSES
BARRY WILKINSON: "We had quite a few problems just getting Harry's glasses right because when he was just a tiny little fellow, he started coming up in these red sort of marks on his face and we found out he was allergic to the material that they made the spectacles out of."

DEFENCE AGAINST THE DARK ARTS FOR BEGINNERS BOOK
MIRAPHORA MINA: "[For] The *Defence Against the Dark Arts for Beginners* book, we collected a reference of books from the '30s, '40s, '50s, children's annuals. We looked at the way they were put together, the style of the illustration."

EDUARDO LIMA: "The binding and the finishing of the book as well. We have a really strong passion for books, and for reference books. And we keep buying loads of books all the time and about anything."

MANDRAKES
NICK DUDMAN: "The Mandrakes, we wanted them to be revolting and horrible, and then of course in the film they added a screeching soundtrack – you know, because the sound of a Mandrake can kill. And those are self-contained animatronic objects with their own batteries, their radio control. So any of the actors could actually handle them. There was a lot of shrieking from the kids because of course you pull this thing out of the pot – it really is wriggling, it really is biting at you. They all had a lot of fun with them. In fact, my biggest problem was making sure that we got all the Mandrakes back."

Harry Potter in the Movies

Harry Potter: The Exhibition is produced by Global Experience Specialists (GES).

Special thanks to Warner Bros. Consumer Products and The Blair Partnership. Warner Bros. Consumer Products, a Warner Bros. Entertainment Company, is one of the leading licensing and retail merchandising organisations in the world.

To learn more about the exhibition, visit us at
www.harrypotterexhibition.com

The *Harry Potter* exhibition programme was developed by Firebrand Live in cooperation with GES and Warner Bros. Consumer Products.
Merchandising by Firebrand Live.
Programme design by Darren Richards.
Edited by Ted Beam.
A portion of photography contributed by Robin Stapley.

Harry Potter: The Exhibition is produced by Global Experience Specialists (GES).

Producer's Note

"Hi, my name is David Barron. I'm one of the producers of the *Harry Potter* film series. On behalf of the many brilliant artists and designers who've worked on the films, we want to thank you for coming to experience *Harry Potter*. We hope you have enjoyed your visit and are inspired by the artistry and craftsmanship of what you've seen. Thanks for visiting, and we invite you to come back again soon to experience *Harry Potter: The Exhibition*."

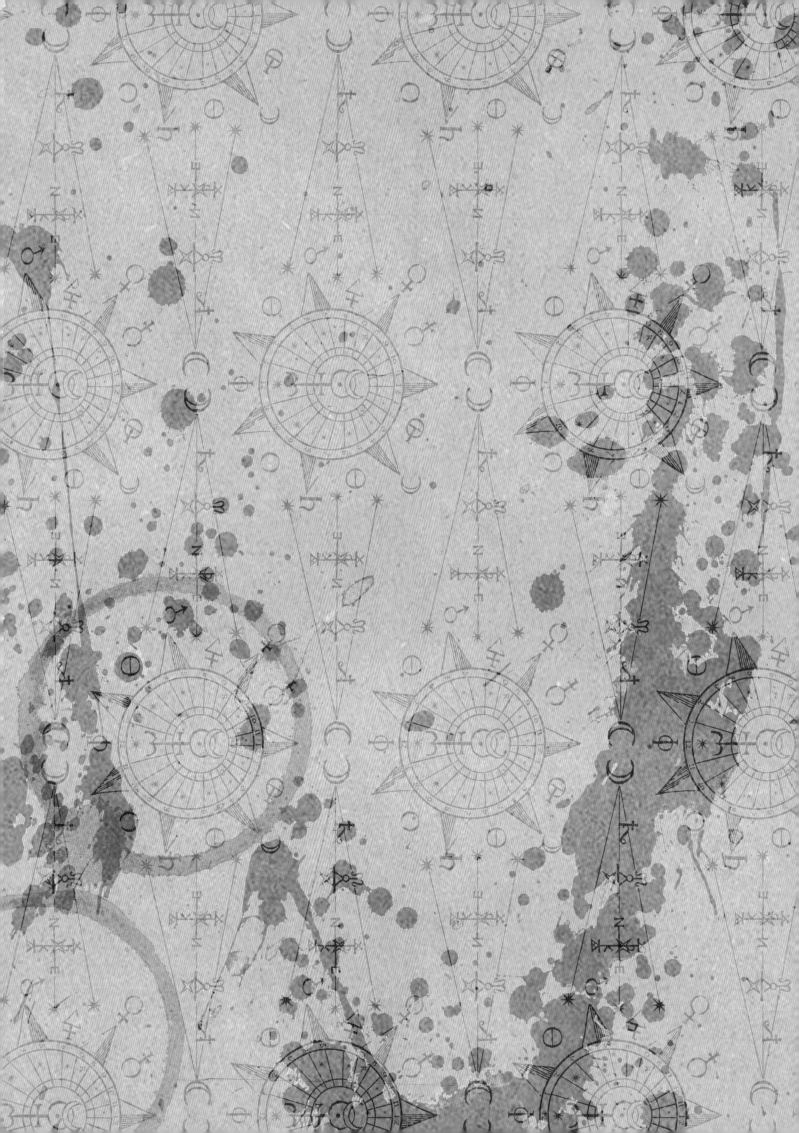